Cover Illustration Copyright © 2015
by Devoree Crist

Cover and Book design
by Mehalet KesateBirhan

Chapter illustrations
by Devoree Crist

Author photograph by Owen Gerald Crist

Paintings are pastels on paper, 2020

Page 6   Zacchaeus
Page 30   Moses and the Burning Bush
Page 46   As A Deer
Page 72   Pentecost
Page 87   Coffee and Cookies with a Friend

Color versions of the illustrations
may be found on the author's website.
http://www.spiritualdirectioninwg.net

Spirit Prayers

Spirit Prayers

*Praying through the time
of pandemic and social unrest*

By Dr. Devoree Clifton Crist

DEDICATION

I dedicate this book to the memory of my incredible parents
Gerald Joseph Clifton and Beatrice Mary Clifton,
who taught me about prayer, compassion and respect,
and how to navigate this world.
Their love and wisdom formed me,
and I miss them very much.

THANKS

I offer gratitude to God for the many wonderful people
who have helped me in the preparation of this book.

Thank you to the Rev. Maren Tirabassi for counsel,
for reading the manuscript and for kind words
and encouragement along the way.

Thanks to Rev. Dr. Clint McCann
for his ongoing support and for being a reader.

I thank Ms. Mehalet KesateBirhan for willingness
to work with me again on a book project.
The layout and cover design are wonderful.

I thank my daughter, Ms. Teresa Crist for proofreading
the manuscript, loving support, and adding humor
to make my work lighter.

I must also thank my family for encouraging me
to keep writing and painting.
These things have helped me greatly
during this time of pandemic.

Special thanks to pastors Rev. Dr. Jacquelyn Foster and
Rev. Clyde Crumpton for taking time out of their
insanely busy schedules to read the book
and offer thoughtful and helpful comments.

Spirit Prayers

Written by Dr. Devoree Clifton Crist

TABLE OF CONTENTS

INDEXES

INTRODUCTION

I am so happy that my first book **Spirit Prayers: Invitations to Worship for Home or Faith Community,** has been so well received. I have received positive feedback about it from both clergy and church leaders and from persons who used it as a personal devotional book. On March 11, 2020 when the city of St Louis issued a social distancing order, we had only heard of one or two cases of Covid-19 in the whole metro area. Shortly thereafter, with rapid spread of the novel coronavirus SARS-CoV-2 across the world and in the United States of America, we found ourselves sheltering in place with cities in lock-down.

Our congregation, like many others, closed the doors to the church building and went to work looking for ways to remain open while socially distanced. We moved online and met virtually using social media and telecommunications software such as Zoom®. It afforded us the opportunity to remain open, to gather as community, and to continue the work of the church in education, preaching and sharing in sacrament, and service. It has been a challenging several months, but the blessings have been many. We found that the only thing that closed for us was our building. The spirit of community was alive. As we worshipped together with a sister congregation we learned that though we missed the intimate setting and physical proximity to our members, there was a sense of belonging and true community that transcended physical closeness. It is different to be sure but in finding this way to stay connected we also found that we are connected more broadly with others.

We have seen an increase in people joining us from a distance.

One way we extended our community time together was by sharing daily prayers. At first the request was to publish online prayers from my book. I offered a few but I soon found that I was called to listen and receive the Word of God from the Holy Scriptures to help us through this difficult time. Scripture offers us so much. We can find within the pages comfort and guidance for living in the world. Spirit Prayers was based on the common lectionary texts used by my pastor or myself in our corporate worship. Spirit Prayers 2 is a response to this very confusing and difficult time of pandemic and social unrest. The prayers you find in this book are a collection of the prayers written for this purpose. The texts are those placed upon my heart from past experience or which were made known to me in reading or heard from various sources that spoke to me. Some of the texts were beloved texts that I go to whenever I need comfort or courage; some were found in the lectionary for that day; others were gifted to me by the Holy Spirit. After reflecting on each text, I wrote a prayer and posted it for the congregation. The scripture verses spoke directly to concerns I was having, to worries and fears I was hearing in my ministry, and to anxiety and uncertainty we are experiencing day to day as a country and in the world.

This virus is mysterious, not fully understood, and highly contagious. It has spread throughout the world and in the United States from the coasts inward. Cases plateaued but after we began to emerge from shut-down, it has surged and shows no indication of stopping. Some are hopeful that vaccines may become available by the end of the year but currently we are setting records for daily numbers of cases reported and concomitant numbers of deaths are continually on the rise. Our time sheltering in place brought about even more concerns, uncertainties and fears. We are still getting mixed messages from our leadership making the situation more chaotic.

In the midst of all of this there is a very frightening disparity among those getting the serious form of the disease. It is disproportionately high in minority populations. The cover has been thrown off underlying racism that has been present in our country since before its founding. The realization of this situation in the dominant culture has caused our country to step back finally and take a good look at injustice. Black and brown people in our country have been sounding the alarm for 400 years but today it appears that people in general are actually paying attention and reacting to the inequities exposed by the virus and captured video of injustices, especially those accompanied by violence that cannot be unseen.

These situations, this stark unveiling of a hard truth, have led to very strong emotional hyperactivity, a pouring out of feelings, tossing us up and down and side to side, some coming all at once.

These prayers are a response to all of this. Scripture has always been a source of steadying, comfort, promise and strength. Scripture provides an outlet for anger, hurt and sadness. I can always find something to soothe my soul. Writing prayers has been one source of centering for me, keeping me calm and energized for the work I do. It is my hope that these texts and prayers might provide hope, comfort, and peace or perhaps be an entry point for your own deep reflection.

I use inclusive language in these prayers. You may see pronouns he/him/his, she/her/hers, and they/them/theirs for God and reference to God as Mother. We are made in God's image and not God in our image. In referencing all our human gender designations in relation to God, we acknowledge that our radically inclusive God is present in each of God's beloved, whoever they may be. Likewise, I use kin-dom in place of kingdom because it is a non-gendered inclusive term for community.

How to use this book

The book is structured to share texts that I have found helpful in this difficult time. Even though there is a lot in this pandemic experience that is unprecedented in the lifetimes of most people on the planet, I have drawn on texts that have helped in the past, and texts that served a struggling people in a very different time but can also speak to this very situation. It is a strong reminder of how God has been and continues to be our help throughout human history. I have organized this book by biblical connections, followed by a section that draws on additional extra-biblical sources. As I mentioned in the introduction, the Bible is a source of comfort and guidance. It is also one of the ways our God offers us peace, hope, love, courage, strength, grace and assurance. The source text is listed with each prayer; I invite you to read the text in your own Bible and if possible, use more than one translation. I also encourage you, if possible, to read it in more than one translation. I have multiple translations of the Bible and even the Hebrew and Greek editions. I find that reading additional interpretations often enriches the hearing of the text, especially if there is something that challenges you in the first reading. Reading the text out loud is also a good way to connect with it. There are several approaches to the material in this book.

- Engage the text, then read the prayer. Use it as an entry into your own deeper prayer.

- Simply read the prayer and use it as the basis for a devotional experience.

- Read them as daily prayers.

- Choose a scripture that you already know and begin there.

- You might find that certain parts of the Bible resonate more with you and spend time in that chapter. I have indicated which texts are found in the lectionary so that you can use the prayers for preaching, liturgical prayers, a study, and so forth.

- Use the prayers as a daily reminder to live your day as worship.

The Gospels

The gospels are the testimony of those who witnessed the life and ministry of Jesus. The words reveal how people experienced the presence of God in the person of Jesus. Within the text are the teachings and the personal faith of Jesus of Nazareth. When times are especially difficult, reading about the courage, deep conviction and faithfulness of Jesus is a great help. The story of Jesus' life and ministry offers us guidelines for a faithful life. He was a follower of the Law and sought to fulfill it in his life. Jesus was passionate about justice because he knew God is just and requires justice in the people. Jesus knew suffering and gave help to those who were in need. He was radically inclusive. And Jesus prayed often.
His passion unto death reflects this commitment to God whom he called Abba or Father, a name which indicates the intimacy of his relationship with God. He taught his followers to pray in the same close and relational way.

Matthew 5:3

Wonderful God who blesses us, reading these blessings from Jesus' Sermon on the Mount reminds us how powerful his words are. In this time of pandemic, we can find ourselves poor in spirit, yet at the end or near the end of our ropes and we turn to you. Please fill us with your Holy Spirit so that our sagging spirits may be lifted up to face these days and nights knowing you are with us. When we are weak you make us strong, when we despair you give us hope, when we are weary you replenish us. Even when we cannot feel your presence you are working to keep us whole until we are revived.

We are grateful for your love and grace, freely given always.

In the name of our teacher, Jesus, we pray, AMEN.

Matthew 5:4

God, source of our being, The second blessing speaks to loss and how we are mourning! There is no getting around it, we must grieve our losses, but it is very hard to grieve in a pandemic when we cannot gather, hug, hold hands, or just have the comfort of another human being next to us. We've lost friends and loved ones, coworkers and others we know, and there have been hundreds of thousands of deaths in our country and around the world from the virus. Black and brown persons suffer most from the disease. On top of this, more people with dark skin are dying at the hands of those we are supposed to trust for our safety. We cry out, O God save us! And you give us what we need to remain strong in the face of all this loss. We trust that Jesus was saying we will be comforted by you when we must mourn. We've lost our sense of security, our jobs, our carefree lives. But even as more people feel and acknowledge the hurt, the suffering, the humiliations, the inhumanity, the cruelty, the evil worked upon our own, there is that spark of hope, that touch of grace, that sense of purpose that keeps us from deep despair. It is in you and with you we will make it through. Please continue to change hearts and fill all of us with Your Holy Spirit to see us through this sad and scary time. In Jesus name we pray, AMEN.

Matthew 5:5

Oh God, with the guiding of your Holy Spirit, make me meek, so that I do not take advantage of anyone. Make me gentle so I will not hurt anyone. Make me weak so I will find strength in you alone. Make me content with who I am so that I will revel in your goodness to me. Make me humble so that I might see the gifts and value of others. In this way I will be rich beyond measure for I will find communion with you and also with my brothers and sisters, your children. And I will have all that I need. In Jesus' name I pray, AMEN.

Matthew 5:6

O God, Source of all that is good in the world, we understand hunger and thirst. This is the body's way to help us survive. We hunger and thirst for you which means we long for righteousness. Righteousness is living in you and you living in us. It is making sure those with physical hunger and thirst are fed and given drinkable water. Your word, O God, is our path. Send your Holy Spirit so that these holy words are etched on our hearts. Show us how to help those who hunger for freedom and safety. On behalf of those who are trying to tell the world what they need, trying to speak truth to power, help us to stand together, hear them and do whatever we can to be in solidarity as Jesus did and still does. Open our eyes and ears to righteous pleas for equal protection, equal treatment and a sense of shalom. Your spirit is on the move. Move us now, for we hunger for righteousness. Show us our part. You have given us gifts to share. Your grace is our strength. We pray for the day when all may be filled. There is enough for all. Let that reality live in us all. In Jesus' name we pray. AMEN.

Matthew 5:7-9

Great God our Mother, these words from Jesus speak to the web of connection that we have in you. When we are merciful, we experience mercy; when we are pure of heart, we see you clearly. When we seek peace, we all experience peace and can share the benefits of being your children, together. In these times when we must as a people cry out at the injustice around us, we know the physical Jesus would be with us at the protest. Jesus is there now, all his words speaking to us to show love, compassion, and mercy. By the power of your Holy Spirit we ask you to change us and help us free ourselves from egotistical, self-centered, controlling tendencies that keep us from hearing the needs of others. Let us live as one family in you, knowing that you love all of us and wish a good life for everyone. AMEN.

Matthew 5:10-12

Savior God, we are fighting a long battle for justice and we know you are with us. You are our hope. Remarkably, this pandemic has been a catalyst for change. As we struggle to contain and manage the coronavirus, that other virus, racism, has been uncovered for many who chose never to acknowledge it. As a nation we are seeing the consequences of systemic institutionalized racism. We are being called to stand up to injustice. With your Holy Spirit on the move within and around us, may we find the courage to be strong in the face of such a formidable opponent. The powers of privilege and greed want to dominate all and refuse to recognize the sacredness of every one of your beloved children. Their resistance is strong but the movement toward justice is also gathering strength. We are grateful for your presence. We ask you to open our leaders' hearts and fill them with compassion. We pray for our country, for all our people, that the protests will lead to positive change, that new relationships will be forged, that we will see justice in the form of equal rights, equal protection, equal access, and equal treatment. Your kin-dom is come when all are welcomed, all are included, all receive love. It sometimes seems impossible, but with you all things are possible. Give us strength. Give us courage. Give us stamina. With the Holy Spirit, and the teaching of our lord Jesus Christ, we will continue to work in every way we can for justice at home and globally. AMEN.

Matthew 6:9-13

Loving parent God, you are ever-present, and your name is holy. We want to be just, love unconditionally, and work so that everyone is provided with what they need to thrive. That is your will, and shows us what the world will look like if we welcome your kin-dom. But we take more than we need and thereby leave others wanting. So we ask you to give us the right heart each day not to seek more for ourselves until others have what they need. Forgive us for our failing to follow Jesus. We promise to forgive others in the same way. With the power of your Holy Spirit we ask that you strengthen us against the pull toward complicity and selfcenteredness. We look to you for a change of heart, a new way of thinking that reflects your will for the whole creation. AMEN.

Matthew 11:28-30

O Holy One, we are feeling fear, anxiety, unease, and perhaps a sense of helplessness. This virus is rapidly spreading, and we already feel its impact on our lives. It frightens us and makes us deeply uneasy that we know so little about it. These are heavy burdens indeed. What a great comfort to know that you carry them with us. We know you are concerned with our wellbeing. You hold us up with grace.
You surround us with love.
You comfort us with hope.
We pray in the name of the one with whom we are yoked, Jesus, the Christ, AMEN.

Matthew13:3-9

God of Wonder, we marvel at the world you created. We are in a season of growing. This is the time when seeds are growing into plants and producing vegetables or fruit or even trees. Jesus' parable of the sower speaks to us in the difficult times we are facing. You have given us your word and we can hear it to live in it, be moved by it, and feel supported by it, or we can struggle against what we are hearing. As seed on the path we allow the things we experience, like this pandemic, to snatch away our ability to experience your presence. As seed on rocky ground we forget how Jesus is our root, a foundation in our lives and find ourselves flailing in the chaos. As seed among thorns we are overcome by racism, sexism or any way treating people as "other." You call us to love our neighbor but that call, that command is choked out by fear and hatred, by the inability to see the other as us and not them. But as the seed on good soil we renew our commitment to you and find in Jesus' teachings a way to be faithful even as our world is changing in ways we never imagined. Grounded by Jesus Christ and with the inflowing of your Holy Spirit we can be transformed by your word and sow the seeds of love in a hurting world. We pray in Jesus' name that this may be so. AMEN.

Matthew 13:16

Generous giving God, you are actively reaching out to us always. You reveal yourself to us in many ways. When we take time to pause and turn our face to you and give ourselves over to you we can see you, we can hear you, we can even taste and smell and touch you in the world. You have gifted us with our senses to know you. In the same loving creative moment, you endowed us with emotion. What a great and wonderful gift, to recognize you in life and love and even in sorrow and suffering. These are the ways your Holy Spirit moves in us to bring us close to you. With great gratitude we pray in Jesus' name, the One who opened the way to you by his life and his teaching. AMEN.

Matthew 13 :24-30

Almighty God, we have been physically separated by pandemic precautions but we remain bound together as your people in your love and grace. We ask you to send us your Holy Spirit to facilitate this sense of community as we navigate a new way of being. We open ourselves to your word, listen for your voice and strengthen our relationship with you. The path we walk is not easy. You provide the seed of guidance, love, and grace to help us, but we are also surrounded by false guides like hatred, greed or worldly desires, promises that pull us from the path or add obstacles in our way. Let us be attentive to the movement of your Holy Spirit as she leads us! Help us to choose the way of Jesus. May your word fortify us especially in this time of struggle These times are hard, we surely need your love and grace. We pray in the powerful name of Jesus, your son, our Lord, AMEN.

Matthew 20:1-16

Generous God, we are so tied to equity when it comes to us but not so much when it comes to others. In the midst of a pandemic it is even more obvious that people can be selfish, without regard to the needs of others. The workers in the parable are getting a pittance really. The daily wage was a subsistence wage. It reminds us that people need a living wage. Those who are suffering the most during the shut down are those whose wages barely meet their needs. God of all, pour your Holy Spirit into us as we consider your Word. Help us to reflect on the inequities in this world. Give us wisdom and compassion so that we might be champions for others. Give us the determination to be a part of your divine mission so that people get what they need not just to survive but to have a good life. Today we pray for strength and courage to open our hearts to your message for us. It is with gratitude for your constant love and care that we pray, in Jesus' blessed name. AMEN.

Matthew 22:34-40

God of Wonder, meditating on the greatest commandments it seems all too simple. If I love you and my neighbor everything is all right. In reality, we are too consumed with our own things to even remember you. We will love our neighbor as long as we get something out of it and we define neighbor in very narrow terms. But we don't want to be that way. Immerse us in your Holy Spirit and dissolve the shell of selfishness in which we live. Then let us continually live in your Spirit so we can experience your boundless love. In response we will see everyone as neighbor and share the love you have given. Loving you and loving neighbor requires an open heart. We open ours to you. We pray with gratitude for Jesus, our teacher, AMEN.

Matthew 27:57-66

O most Holy God, when Jesus was killed by crucifixion, those who would silence his message did all they could to kill the movement as well as the man. Today we still struggle with your message. Racism, ageism, sexism, and oppression of all kinds are very evident in this time of pandemic. O God break open all our hearts and free our minds to know and understand your mission. Help us to keep the movement Jesus began alive. Let the desire for justice be the starting point for our lives. Let everything we are, we do, and we say be rooted in your love for all. AMEN.

Matthew 28:1-10

Holy Loving God, thank you for your unending love. Thank you for your son who gives us a way to you. We celebrate the resurrection in great joy because despite all the fear, anxiety, sorrow, pain, suffering, and injustice in the world, you are in the midst of it all, and that gives us great hope. We see you in so many ways lighting our lives. Your holy presence gives us strength and the will to do what we can to make this world a better place. Immerse us in your Spirit as we hear the message of resurrection and what it still means today in this place, in this time. You are with us. Your love makes us whole. Your love heals. In the name of the Risen Christ we pray, Alleluia, AMEN.

Mark 1:35-39

O God, Our Guide and Director, Jesus went to you in prayer before he went into the field and worked. Without you our efforts are empty and without meaning. And so we ask for the counsel of your Holy Spirit. In all we do, in all we say, and in all our living in this world we need you.

We need your light to find our way in this time of uncertainty.
We need your hope so we don't sink into depression and despair.
We need your grace to find our place in the world.
We need your love to know how to best use the gifts you have given for the betterment of this world.
We need your truth to be one with you in mind and spirit.
We need your compassion to make sure all or our brothers and sisters have care.
We pray as Jesus prayed. AMEN.

Mark 4:10-12 (see also Isa 6:8-11)

Blessed Jesus, you gave us the secret of God's empire. When we care for the poor and seek justice for all, it comes alive. Come Holy Spirit, open our hearts wide and fill us with the compassion, justice, mercy, and love we need to participate in the Holy knowledge. We want to look and see, hear and understand, and be an active part of a just and compassionate world that can flourish even in the face of pandemics.

We wish this for all humankind because God forgives and we all have the capacity, with your abundant grace, to turn our lives around. AMEN.

Mark 4:35-39

God our hope, we are being thrown about on a raging sea. We are frightened by the intensity of the storm and uncertain about the outcome. We feel the wind coming from many directions. We don't want to die from a viral infection but we are afraid of losing our ability to survive without work. We are also weary from systemic racism causing so many unnecessary deaths and struggles. We find the stress of doing nothing or trying to do far too much is tearing at us like lashing waves. We also feel the burden of grieving at a distance, suffering alone, feeling isolated. This storm of emotions is harsh and unexpected. Let the wind of your Holy Spirit guide our fragile boats. Let the raging storm inside become calm.

Save us, O God, help us find serenity in this chaos. AMEN.

Mark 4:39-40

O God, we are in a raging storm. We cannot see the light, many have fallen. We need you now, we cry to you to wake up. We want to put our trust in you, but the fear is overwhelming sometimes. Please send your Holy Spirit, the Comforter, to open our ears so we will listen and hear your calming voice saying, "Why are you afraid? Don't you know I am with you? Where is your faith?" Strengthen our faith O God! AMEN.

Mark 5:25-34

Loving God, we have been feeling the weight of the pandemic and discord in the country for many months now. Fear, worry, and anxiety are constant companions even as we go about the usual activities of daily living. We reach out to you for healing knowing that one touch from your Holy Spirit will calm and soothe our souls. The sense of dread will fall away and we will find our way. We will get through this because you are near. AMEN.

Mark 6:30-44

O Most Holy God, we honor and praise you. We put our trust in you. We know that your promise always to be with us is true and your love is steadfast. You fed your people in the wilderness, you fed the five thousand, and you feed us now. We are nourished through your Holy Spirit who moves in and among us. O God, thank you for life in the Spirit. Open us to your Spirit now as we find ourselves hungering for you in a strange and difficult time. Give us the food of compassion, of understanding, of patience, of unselfishness. We pray earnestly for all those who suffer from Covid-19. We pray for their families and caregivers. We pray for those who come in contact with them. We pray for those tirelessly working on treatment and a vaccine. We pray for all those who are working to keep things going, the essential workers. We pray for people returning to work where many still do not take the pandemic seriously.

We pray in the holy name of Jesus, AMEN.

Luke 6:17-19

God of Springtime and new growth, we've seen the earth wake up from its winter sleep and produce blossoms and greening of the trees and grass. Likewise, we have seen the measured reopening of our cities. We are also seeing the awakening of many people to the very real inequities in this country. We seek your healing for all that ails us. We, like the people in the crowd trying to touch Jesus, long for your Holy Spirit. Sickness and death from the coronavirus are still on the rise. Systemic racism underlies everything in our society. We are feeling the effect of prolonged shutdown, social isolation, and fear. Things are changing rapidly, and we call to you. Embrace us all with the power of your Spirit and heal the world. Give us the stamina to continue. We pray in Jesus' name, AMEN.

Luke 6:20

Precious Savior, you came into the world in poverty to show us how God is the God of the marginalized. This understanding of God is present throughout the Holy Scripture. We open ourselves to you and to the movement of your Holy Spirit in, through, and among us, surrounding us with grace. We have an opportunity to reevaluate our own world view as we step back from life as we know it in this time of forced sheltering in place. Help us to bring our view of the world into sync with yours so that we, too, will be in solidarity with the poor and marginalized. Realizing the truth that we are all your children to be loved and respected and seen, we will experience the kin-dom of God. Thank you, Jesus, for your love and teaching and for your companionship on the journey. AMEN.

Luke 9:23-25

O God most high, Jesus said take up your cross and follow me. Taking up a cross sounds terrifying but what is it that the cross signifies? Why did Jesus go to the cross? It was all about being faithful to you. You abhor injustice and you hold all your children as equal and loved. Jesus defied the powers that be, lifting up your reign over the rulers of the time - a reign where all have what they need to thrive. We ask you now, what can we do? Are we capable of being bearers of justice in an unjust world? Yes, with the help of your Holy Spirit we can. The road is not easy but giving all we have for the sake of Christ is the way to truly be your people and bring about your kin-dom on earth. Fill us with your Spirit and help us find our true selves. We pray as followers of Jesus Christ, AMEN.

Luke 12:16-21

Creator God, we thank you for everything we have.
You created the earth and all that is in it. You lovingly put us here and provide all we need for a full life. Unfortunately, so many of us have become self-centered and greedy. Our society values success by possessions and we have forgotten that everything is yours. Jesus reminds us that we are to share what we have because it is in our support and care for each other that we find the greatest treasure. This is what connects us to you. In this time when many are in trouble, the need to share what we have been given is extremely important. So, we ask that by the indwelling of your Holy Spirit you shake us up and open our hearts to the importance of love, especially for those in need. It is in love that we participate in your mission for the earth. AMEN.

Luke 14:34-35

Holy God, salt is a preserving agent and a seasoning. Our faith is like salt, it gives meaning and flavor to our lives. If salt loses its flavor of what use is it? So, too, without our relationship to you we are nothing. We feel lost and alone. With the instilling of your Holy Spirit strengthen our faith. Let us be always loyal and true to you. We pray, AMEN.

Luke 24:13-49

We praise you, O magnificent God. We experience the presence of Christ in those around us if we take the time to truly see and hear them. As we socially distance ourselves, we are finding new ways to encounter each other, and we pray that you will bless us with your Spirit moving in and through us to stir us to action. By your grace let us remember and carry on the work Jesus began. Like the disciples on the road to Emmaus, let our hearts burn within us. When we encounter others let our lives show the joy, hope, and wellbeing that comes from experiencing and following Jesus. We pray in his name, AMEN.

Luke 24:44-50

O Blessed Jesus, thank you for your words spoken, your teaching, your time on this earth opening minds, feeding people, feeding souls. You are the Christ, the Messiah. You sent the gift of the Holy Spirit so we would not be alone. We imagine the joy the disciples experienced being with you again, their teacher, and the awe they must have felt as you ascended. Even now, rereading those words reminds us how much God has given. Please open us to the Scripture, open us to the Holy Spirit, open us to the marvelous love of God. We receive the Holy Spirit into our being and with grace we can persevere through these unsettling and uncertain times and find light in the darkness. AMEN

John 10:1-10

O Holy Shepherd who guides a flock whose members easily stray, you call us each by name and open the gate.
Gather us today in the circle of your care. If we put our trust in you, we know you will not fail us. You will provide all we need to be whole. Help us to be attentive to your word.
It is with gratitude that we accept your claim on us as individual Christians. We are yours now and into eternity. Please pour your Holy Spirit in us so that we might be revived and renewed in our commitment to you. It is in Jesus' wonderful name that we pray, AMEN.

John 12:1-11

God, Source of our being, it feels appropriate to be sitting with Mary, Martha, Lazarus, and Jesus at a meal. The siblings fed and anointed him showing their love and concern for one who was their close friend but also their savior. We, too, welcome Jesus and acknowledge his ministry of love and concern for the poor. We ask that you put your Holy Spirit into us so that we might find our way in this frightening time. Heal us. Rescue us. Save us. With Jesus as our guide we pray that we may find a path out of this upsetting, disturbing, and disorienting time to arrive at a better way of being, more aligned with you. AMEN.

John 13:21-25

Forgiving God, how often I betray you, even if not consciously! By my unkind thoughts towards others; When I try to blame you and ask, "Where are you?" knowing full well you are here with me. By my desire to take a different path from the one you so clearly illuminate for me. Although you are aware of how I turn from you or ignore you, or think I know better than you, yet you still love me with a love that is immeasurable. You forgive me, nurture me, put your Spirit in me and strengthen me for the path. Please send your Holy Spirit now. Intensify my faith. Build up my courage. Help me to stay the course and not stray. Help me to remember that you bring good into any situation. Help me to see you in the midst of this troubling time. In Jesus' name I pray, AMEN.

John 14:1-14

O Holy God we say we trust in you. We know that you are always near and ready when we turn to you, just like a loving parent caring for their child. There are times when we feel helpless or plowed under by circumstances that we cannot seem to overcome; yet especially then you find us and care for us. Your covenant is true, and you are faithful always. We know Jesus and through him we know you. This sacred relationship we have with you is unfailing, but we still struggle. We ask you to take your frightened children into your embrace and nurture our growing, sometimes faltering, faith through the indwelling of your Holy Spirit. It is by your grace that we will find the depth of faith to trust in you completely. We can trust you will guide and show us our path as protests around the country speak truth to power. It is your truth they speak; that life has value, that we need to bring all our brothers and sisters to the table, that everyone is a human being deserving of life abundant. In this exciting, though unnerving time, O God, keep the fire we are experiencing lit so we do not tire but stay the course. Let us shape the world you have called us to make, a world where everyone can breathe free and find a safe and good life. We pray this with the assurance of Jesus Christ, AMEN.

John 14:15-21

Eternal God, when Jesus left his disciples he promised that he would not leave them as orphans but that you would send the Holy Spirit as a Companion, an Advocate. As we are in the midst of a seemingly unending pandemic, your Holy Spirit does indeed move in, among, and through us, making us able to be powerful companions and advocates for others. When we stand in solidarity with others who are marginalized and have no voice, we become bringers of the kin-dom, healers of the breach, and your presence in this world. When we stand in solidarity with those who suffer disproportionately in this pandemic we show your truth, your power, and above all your love in a hurting world. This is the reason Jesus came to us. We seek to follow him by keeping his commandments to love you and to love our neighbor. We ask you to continue to send your Holy Spirit into our lives to rouse us to love in action. AMEN.

John 14:25-26

Yes, Compassionate God, you send your Holy Spirit to us as a teacher at Jesus' request. In this text Jesus tells us we are not alone. You strengthen and guide us in that knowledge by the grace of the Holy Spirit showered upon us every day. May Jesus' words resonate in us, awaken and rouse us to full faithful lives. He taught us how to live. By following Jesus, we can and will make a difference in the world. Your constant presence is our stability, our balance, even in chaos. In Jesus' name we pray, AMEN.

John 20:19-31

O God of renewal and rebirth, we continue to bask in the warmth of resurrection love. Those who first encountered the Risen Christ were astonished and filled with joy.
But Thomas needed to see Jesus with his own eyes and touch him. Today our faith is put to the test with this pandemic. Though we claim to know that you are trustworthy and faithful, we can find ourselves wondering if you are really there. By the inpouring of your Spirit strengthen our faith. Melt away doubt and give us hope as we navigate this frightening time. We worship and pray in Jesus' holy name, Alleluia, AMEN.

Hebrew Bible
except Psalms

It might be astonishing to find how much of the Hebrew Bible is present in the Gospels. We shouldn't be surprised since Jesus and his followers were Jews. Jesus knew the scriptures and studied them. His theology was formed in these Scriptures and he was true to their message. It is the same message that he thought had been corrupted by the Scribes and Pharisees. His teachings were meant to return the people to the truth, to the real meaning of those Scriptures. The message was that God is love. God is just and merciful and requires justice and love in the people – the people of God. The texts I share here reflect this message, a message that is still profoundly true for us. We can trust in God knowing that we are loved. As we are bound to God we naturally will live a life of love and justice, caring for one another, receiving strength and courage from God to make that not only possible but inevitable. Studying and reflecting on the texts that Jesus used in his life enriches our understanding of him and offers insight into his teachings, his absolute trust in God and the way we can rely on God to be actively present in our lives.

Genesis 1:26-27

O God, your ever-flowing love and grace are abundant and available to everyone. You hold each one dear. No one is left out of your embrace. You are One who gives life. You are the air we breathe, the water we need, the blood circulating in our veins. You, O God, are life. You are the love that binds us one to another in one body. You created us in your image and so we ask that you open us to your Holy Spirit so that we can see you in others. When we allow your love to touch us deeply and then share love with all that we encounter, we will find the unity you desire. When we all are one family loving you, loving each other as we are, and loving the earth and all you created, then we will know the fullness of life in you. Break open our hearts and open our minds to this way of being. We ask this in the name of Jesus, the Christ, AMEN.

Genesis 2:7

Creator God, you breathed your own life into us to make us who we are. It is your Holy Spirit within us that gives us life. During this long lasting time of chaos and disquiet marked by uncertainty and fear, we look to our center for help. You are always there and on that we can depend. AMEN.

Genesis 6:5-8

Forgiving and supportive God, it is not unusual for some to think that a horrific occurrence is related to wickedness in the world. We remember the story of Noah and your grief at the evil you saw. You must be grieving now. It is good for us to consider how greed and hatred, if left unchecked, soon dominate the way of life. We have become lax in our active call to challenge such things. The pandemic has unveiled the evil in our world. As followers of Christ we are called to be healers, reconcilers, and caregivers. Strengthen your people, O God, and with the power of your Holy Spirit in us we will do what we can to improve the world by working together to survive the pandemic and the evil of racism, hatred, and greed which, like the virus, threaten us all. AMEN.

Genesis 22:1-14

God, you who ask us to walk humbly with you, we look at the story of Abraham and Isaac and are shocked at such a request and even more shaken by the level of faith Abraham showed to obey you. How often we say we trust you and we will be faithful only to stumble when our faith is tested. Being aligned with your will can be very hard especially in a society that values money and power over compassion, mercy, and love. Please pour your Holy Spirit into each of us, so we might understand this story in light of how you sent your own son, Jesus, into the world. He is our root and we bloom out into the world firmly grounded in your love. We can trust your love to see us through anything and everything. In Jesus' name we pray, AMEN.

Exodus 1:8 – 2:10

God, caregiver of the people, you are the Saving God because, despite all of Pharaoh's attempts to limit and harm your people, your people survived. Enslavement with cruel and grueling work to oppress didn't stop the people from multiplying. Attempted male infanticide didn't work because the midwives loved you and trusted in your promise. This is true even today. There are evil ones among us trying to oppress and even kill your people, but your love is spread through those who love you and your people survive. As we see a growing movement to respect and protect the lives of all your beloved, we know that it is love that will continue to move your people to justice and peace. We ask you to shower your Holy Spirit upon your people today as we strive to remain connected in new and innovative ways. We recall that nothing can keep us from your love. Even a pandemic will not keep your people from being your people. By your steadfast love give us hope for the healing of your world. AMEN.

Exodus 3:1-5

God of the burning bush, you told Moses he was standing on Holy Ground. Your presence makes any place holy. You were with the Israelites in the wilderness and did not leave them when they entered the promised land. You remained with them through exile and you have never abandoned your people, even sending your son incarnate into the world. We know you are still with us today, ever-present, ever-faithful, and active in our lives. We gather to worship in a virtual setting but each place we are is still holy because you are present. We ask you to bring the hope of the Holy Spirit into our hearts and souls wherever we may be to assure us of your presence even in the midst of this difficult season, a time of struggle, a time of uncertainty. In your Holy Spirit we are one community worshipping you in holy places for you are here with us. We are standing on holy ground. AMEN.

Exodus 17:1-7

Most Patient God, you hear the moans and groans of your people in the wilderness and today. Some cry "Where are you?" Others say, "Help us!" while others cry out, "If you love us, why did you lead us here?" We find ourselves in an unanticipated situation. Like those in the wilderness we turn to you, complaining, and your response is unrestrained love. You give us what we need - a reminder that we are all in this together, that you are with us through it all, that we have the ability and means to care for one another, and that you give us the strength and courage to do so even in the midst of hardship. Through pandemic, death, fires, hurricanes, strange weather patterns, melting ice caps, pour the blessing of the Holy Spirit into us like a river flowing into the ocean. This is the water for our thirst, flowing steadily from you in our direction. You are with us. Let us hear your word, seek you daily, and share in praise and gratitude for all you have done for us. We pray in Jesus' name, AMEN.

Exodus 20:1-20

O Most Holy God, you yourself gave the ten commandments to your people through Moses. Jesus summed them up by saying "You must love the Lord your God with all your heart, with all your being, and with all your mind and you must love your neighbor as you love yourself. All the Law and the Prophets depend on these two commands." We understand this to be true and vital for in Jesus Christ we find that loving you means loving each other. They go hand in hand. We ask you to send your Holy Spirit to move in, around, and through us. We will receive her, living in you, loving you fully, receiving your love, and releasing that love to the world. AMEN.

Exodus 32:33-35

Loving Parent God, we praise you! When we look to Exodus we understand that people wanted to make sense of their lives. They knew that they had fallen short with that golden calf and when the plague came to them, they just knew that it was a punishment from you. We may get caught up in a "why?" because of this pandemic today. We were caught totally off guard by it and struggle to explain it, why now, why us, why the whole world? It is probably a good thing to look at how we have not been caring for each other or the world, how we might DESERVE a "plague." As a nation we certainly have fallen short in our response to care for one another. Our situation is the result of greed, self-centeredness, a lack of preparation, and an unwillingness to sacrifice for the good of us all. But you, O God, are compassionate, and we know that you don't cause these things but rather share our experiences of pain, sorrow, and anguish, all because of your amazing love for us. You hold us when we are afraid and assure us that you are very much present. We thank and praise you for the gift of your Holy Spirit who pours out your love and grace on us every day. Let your spirit that dwells in us rouse us into greater compassion and a sense that we belong to one another in you. AMEN.

Joshua 1:1-7

God who saves, we know the story of how you delivered your people out of Egypt, out of slavery. You gave the law to protect them and land so they would survive. You spoke to Joshua as they entered the promised land and did not leave them. We hear your promise today. We know you are here with us. We are in the midst of a pandemic and our survival depends on watching out for each other. As followers of Christ we are called to care and love. So please kindle the fire of your Holy Spirit within us and stir up compassion so that we are all part of the plan to be safe again. When we use precautions, we are loving our neighbors. Just as you set forth the law you gave to Moses to help the community care for one another, we must also care for one another by being safe. Jesus understood your law was all about love when he said that the greatest commandments were to love you and love each other. Then he gave his new we can stay on the path and endeavor to love as Jesus did. In His name we pray, AMEN.

Proverbs 3:5

Holy One, we struggle with this one. We trust in you. We really do. But there is always that desire for control that pops up. We need your Spirit to reside in us and to guide us, because we know we will not think clearly without you. Yet, how many times have we all turned to other sources including ourselves for insight and forgotten to seek you first! At times like these where we are faced with totally unexpected challenges that test us, we seek to make sense of it by our own means, and the result is disorder and confusion and bewilderment. We fall into chaos but in you we find focus. In that centeredness, we experience hope and direction. We turn to you, now. Help us find our way. AMEN.

Proverbs 14:31

God of the powerless, we implore you to remake us in your Holy Spirit so we are the ones who are kind and not the exploiters or worse, the uncaring. As we reflect on our own way of thinking during this strange season of the coronavirus we ask you to open our minds and our hearts to the powerless. We confess that at times we completely ignore those not in our immediate circle. Maybe during this time of forced confinement, we can let your Spirit in to guide our worldview. Let our strength be the strength of the most vulnerable. We ask this in the name of Jesus, the Christ, who was one with the poor and the unwanted. AMEN.

Ecclesiastes 1:9-10

Eternal God, this text, attributed to Solomon, who in his old age thought that all was pointless, that the life of a human is short and insignificant, reminds us that as a species we make the same mistakes over and over. We tend not to learn from the past. The situation we are in is an example. We have experienced viral infections of great magnitude before, yet we were not prepared for this one. We are shocked by this new experience, which reminds us that we are often short sighted and self-centered. But God, you are with us through it all, offering wisdom and grace. We ask that you send your Holy Spirit into our midst and give us hope and understanding. Help us to learn from this difficult time to respect nature, acknowledge our weakness, and try to be a stronger community throughout the world. Help us to recognize our shared humanity and care for each other and the earth. AMEN.

Song of Solomon (Also called Song of Songs) 2: 8-13

God of All, you are love and in our experiences of love in the world we find you. Nothing is more like your pure love than our intimate relationship with another. That is why this beautiful song to one's beloved is a reflection on something sacred. God, we find you immersed in our lives, not only in corporate worship, but in those everyday encounters with people, with nature, and when we choose to love and accept ourselves. You are present in all aspects of our living. We meet you in joy, sorrow, fear, concern, uncertainty. We are grateful for your Holy Spirit moving among, in, around, and through us. It is by your love that we are able to overcome, survive, and recover after struggle. Help us to be open to your tender, dynamic, and transforming love. When we let you in, we are filled with the understanding that we are not alone, and this might move us to sing a song of holy pure love. AMEN.

Isaiah 29:18-19

O precious God, how many times have we been deaf and blind to your word, to your presence? We often fail to see you in the poor and disenfranchised. We forget the core message of the gospels, to love one another. As we are again confronted with the inequities in our systems accentuated during this pandemic, we remember how Jesus, facing those same injustices, gave his life, even unto death, to save the world. Jesus was passionate, an activist, a feminist, a healer, bringing your reign of peace, equality, and justice into the world. We cannot let his ministry lose its meaning. We must do likewise. Our lives should be directed toward justice. Our greatest joy will come when those who are suffering and hungry, in need of shelter, medicine, and safety can rejoice. We know this is your desire for us. Let us embrace your Holy Spirit within us and follow Jesus. AMEN.

Isaiah 43:19

God of Glory, today we pray for the church and for the world. Something is stirring in us. Please make us anew. We want to be your church, we want to be your offspring who offer our lives in service. We want to practice justice, to seek it every day of our lives. It is hard with all the pressures from the outside. But with your Holy Spirit on the inside, deep within us, guiding and strengthening us, we can and will follow Jesus and honor you. And so, we pray for our church leaders, our pastors, and ourselves. With your help we can be the church alongside others who know and love you. We pray also for our planet and all the people of the world. We have seen a new view of the humanity of others and the value of the earth. Those who have be unseen and unheard are being acknowledged. We pray that through us you will change the world. You are indeed doing something new! AMEN.

Ezekiel 37:11-14

God of renewal and growth, you spoke through Ezekiel to the Israelites saying, "I will put my Spirit in you and you will live." In this time and place, wherever we are, we worship you. We ask you again to breathe into us your Holy Spirit. We move through a wilderness realizing that life is pale and meaningless, nothing but dry bones without you. Open our hearts and minds to receive what you lovingly offer - your own self to make us whole. In Jesus' name we pray. AMEN.

Amos 5:21-24

Source of our being, we turn to your word from the prophet Amos. We are finding ourselves in a time of wilderness, seeking you, wanting to know you, wanting to be known by you. It is a time of remembering why we are church. Amos tells it like it is. Do we gather to be seen for our ego's sake or to be seen by you? Do we make your face known in the world by acts of justice and care? Do we show our love for you by receiving and loving all without reservation? Do we act superficially for show or deeply with compassion for the other? O God of All, we need your Holy Spirit surrounding us and within us, moving us to live with absolute love for you. We need to receive your love and to respond by passing on your love and justice to the world, especially now in this very difficult time. Open our hearts and minds, our eyes and ears to know what you require of us. We will listen and respond as disciples of Jesus, in whose name we pray. AMEN.

Micah 6:6-8

Great companion God, we try so many times to do our own thing. We imagine that being your children requires great sacrifice and grand deeds, huge gifts to the church, fancy worship services or other such things. The problem is that if we don't do these things, we think we are not being faithful. At the same time, we pass by the homeless person without a thought, we ignore the fact that there is so much food insecurity around us, we disregard racist comments or acts, we pay no heed to the disrespect of women in the workplace or elsewhere, we turn our heads when someone is being bullied or, worse, we laugh at them. So much injustice is silently observed. The prophets remind your people then and now that you aren't interested in splendid acts of praise if we are not also doing our acts of justice. You want us to be kind and caring and loving. And you want us to recognize that you walk with us so that we are never alone, never without support, never "on our own." You send your Holy Spirit as a trusted friend with outstretched hand inviting us to walk with you. We accept and give our lives to you. We will do justice and love kindness. AMEN.

Habakkuk 1:2-4

Almighty and merciful God, Habakkuk could have been a Black Lives Matter activist. These words ring out in our day. All across our country we are seeing peaceful protests marred by violence. While protesting injustice, those marching are exposed to it, as their rights are challenged. There is an effort to shut down their voices and yet they continue to cry out. Speaking truth to power is never easy or completely safe. But we have Jesus, whose passion for justice never faltered even when the power structure sought to silence him. In Jesus we can find strength; we can persevere; we can fight for justice. Please nourish us with your Holy Spirit, so that we will be able to sustain our call for justice in the face of oftentimes violent resistance. Like Habakkuk we complain but we also know, as he did, that we can call you and you will listen. Have mercy on your people, give us sustenance for the work, revive us when we falter, and let us rejoice in even small victories. Help us find joy in the fact that more and more people are acknowledging the sin of racism. We offer gratitude for our Lord Jesus with whom we are yoked for the long difficult road ahead. AMEN.

The Psalms

This book of the Bible gets special treatment because I find I've gone readily and often to these beautiful psalms in this time of pandemic. Actually, when I am feeling a need for a boost or want to shout out my praise and gratitude, I turn to the Psalms. They are a great source of connection with God. The Psalms are songs written for worship in different settings. They represent the many concerns and prayers of the community. The Psalms are particularly helpful in times of duress and emotional pain. The Psalms reflect anger, concern, or a feeling that God is not present. The psalmist cries out to God in misery, woe, grief, worry, and anxiety. We all experience times like this. We also want to express the trust we have in God, the deep love of God we feel, or gratitude for God's presence in our lives. The Psalms offer words for those feelings and also words of relief or release, reminders of God's faithfulness and acknowledgement of who God is in our lives.

Psalm 6:1-6

O My God! How many times do we say those words? But you are our God and we look to you in this time of worry and anxiety and fear. The psalmist pleads for your return, thinking you are gone. Our intention is to be faithful people, but we are being preyed upon by persistent fear and helplessness. People are dying. We need your Holy Spirit to help us live with these emotions but not give in to them. Day by day as we become increasingly weary, the predators see our weakness and, like the psalmist, we wonder if we will survive. But you, O God, are our strength and we will get through this, with your steadfast love to sustain us. AMEN.

Psalm 8

God, Sovereign, your reign is over all creation. You are mighty, grand, marvelous, and all-powerful. Yet you care for each of us as precious children. We are so insignificant in the scheme of creation, but, in your infinite love and compassion, you have given us elevated status and dominion, caretaker status for your world. As we gather as church, socially distanced but very present to one another, we pause to think how we have failed to love the creation as you do. We fight amongst ourselves instead of caring for one another as family. We deplete natural resources without renewing them. We pollute the air and water doing harm to the creatures and plant life on our home planet. We need your Holy Spirit. This is why we ask you to send your Spirit as you have before. Set our hearts on fire to be the people you want us to be, filled with grace, transformed and faithful. With Jesus as our guide we pray, AMEN.

Psalm 12:5-6

Almighty God, you are indeed standing with the poor and
the needy who are oppressed. This is the message of the Holy
Scriptures. Jesus came to us as a child in a very poor family.
He taught us to be in solidarity with those on the outside, the
marginalized, those who are powerless in the world's terms. It
is in understanding that we are all one people, your people, that
we find our true selves belonging to one another and in union
with you. Please let your Holy Spirit encamp in us so that
we will be made compassionate and loving. When we see the
statistics about who are the most vulnerable to the coronavirus
we are also seeing our shortcomings as true followers of Jesus.
Open our eyes, our ears, our minds, and our hearts to the needs
all around us. Let us do all we can to live as one and care for
each other. We pray especially for the courage to use wealth,
resources, and privilege to build up the whole body of Christ.
We pray in Jesus' name, AMEN.

Psalm 13

The Psalmist cries out to you, saying "show yourself."
O God, we cry out to you, too. Help us to see your amazing presence
In those who are working on the front lines to care for the sick,
In those who are making the hard decisions for our safety,
In those who are practicing social distancing,
In those who are buying groceries for the elderly,
In those offering kind words, care, or comfort.
Protect them, O great caregiver.
Yes, you are visible, you are actively present.
Send your Spirit to fill us with the hope that knowing you brings.
Your steadfast love is always with us. AMEN.

Psalm 18:1-3

Source of all, you truly are our strength, our rock, our fortress.
There is so much fear. There is suffering.
Even as we pray, gun sales are rising in our cities.
People are trying to profit from hoarding supplies.
Stay at home orders are necessary because people won't take precautions.
As a nation we are bracing for the worst, and leadership is lacking.
There are many, many reasons for fear.
Help us to accept our fear and recognize your grace.
Your presence is noticeable
In the many attempts to maintain community,
In those who are caring for the sick,
In those preparing for the peak,
In those working to find a treatment or a vaccine,
In grocery workers,
In the beauty of creation all around,
In music,
In the eyes of our loved ones,
In our ability to care for others in so many ways.
We ask you to open our eyes, ears, our minds, our hearts to your Holy Spirit.
Fill us and use us to be your healing in this world.
Help us to find ways to be kind, to reach out to others so that isolation isn't so hard, and everyone realizes that we are in this together.
Heal us O God, Heal our world. AMEN.

Psalm 22: 1-5

Almighty and Merciful God, these words from the psalmist were words our Lord prayed on the cross. He turned to the tradition for a strong and heartfelt plea. We find ourselves in a very scary situation where our enemy is an infectious agent. Something so tiny that can bring us to our knees terrifies us. Will it hurt someone I love; will it kill me? Can we find a cure, a vaccine? We resonate with Jesus' pleading "why?" And like Jesus we turn to you and trust in your wisdom. Our hope is in you. Whatever happens we are in your hands, and, in your hands, we are surrounded by your Holy Spirit. Heal our nation and the world and let this shared experience bring us closer to one another. In you we can and will endure. AMEN.

Psalm 23, John 10:1-10

O Holy Shepherd who guides a flock whose members easily stray, you call us each by name, and open the gate. We put our trust in you as you lead us through the valley of fear and anxiety during the pandemic. It seems so dark because we know so little and the mixed messages we get confuse us even more. But you are with us in our unease, like the shepherd in the psalm moving us through dark and frightening paths with the rod of love and staff of hope gently guiding our way. It is with gratitude that we accept your claim on us as individual Christians. We are yours. With your Holy Spirit living in us, moving us, we will be revived and renewed in our commitment to you. Open our minds and hearts to your counsel. Calm our spirits, ease our anxiety and move us to action as we are able. It is in Jesus' wonderful name that we pray, AMEN.

Psalm 23

The Lord is my shepherd, takes care of me, leads me, even through the dark valley. What comfort I take in the goodness of the One who gives life! We put our trust in you, Good Shepherd, as you lead us through this valley. Sometimes you show up in the form of good people reaching out to care for others. We see love pour out of many people in these troubling days. It is a sign that you are with us, in our unease. With your Holy Spirit guiding our steps we can navigate the hard places and find our way. Open our minds and hearts to your counsel. Calm our spirits, ease our anxiety and move us to act as we are able. AMEN.

Psalm 27:1

You are our everything, loving Parent God. We run to you and find strength in your love. In a pandemic fear is natural. The movement of your Holy Spirit in and among us brings the gift of fear which allows us to react in a productive way. Because we have your grace we can deal with fear as a companion rather than the devourer of our souls. You are our light and our salvation. What is there that can separate us from you? Nothing! So we embrace our fear and use that energy to protect ourselves and others. In Jesus the Christ we are one with you. AMEN.

Psalm 31:15-16

Today I open my heart and soul to you, my beloved God. Let your grace shine upon me like the light and warmth of the sun. I give myself to you completely and ask that, by the power of your Holy Spirit, I might be stilled and centered so I can serve you faithfully even as I maneuver through this strange and difficult time. Yes, as the psalmist says, my times are in your hand, deliver me from the turmoil within. I welcome your love. I am ready to receive it! AMEN.

Psalm 33:20-22

Holy One, you bring us hope. In a time when our lives have been upended, and, for some, devastated, we still have hope because you love us. Even in loss, we can claim your care and comfort and know that all is not lost. We will get through this, though we are all affected by it. We pray that by instilling your Holy Spirit in us, we who are struggling will survive with strength and courage. We pray that those of us privileged only to suffer inconvenience are made to see deeper inequities and choose to help others and make a difference with what we have been given. We pray that all those who have lost someone in this pandemic will be able to grieve their loss. We pray that all those who are keeping this country running by their commitment to do their jobs even as the virus threatens them daily, remain safe. We pray that the racism here is dismantled as more people are willing to recognize everyone as a human being deserving of love and the means to thrive in this rich country. God, you are our hope, it is only through opening ourselves to you that we will understand what it means to love and be loved. AMEN.

Psalm 34:1-3

O God, Creator with unbridled love for all, we praise you!
You are always with us and we give you thanks.
Even when we stray from the path, your love lights our way.
You are amazing, wonderful, kind, loving, and playful.
You make us feel loved and treasured, and we love you back.
When we open ourselves to your Spirit we feel the warmth
and joy that is you! We sing your praise forever!
We pray in Jesus' name, AMEN.

Psalm 34:4-8

God in the trenches, the psalmist reminds us to seek you
in our need. The idea of your angel encamped with us is so
beautiful. It helps us to look for you in the midst of our fears.
When we are crying out for help, help is often right where
we are: in nature, in our own gifts, in those who share our
concerns, in our family, in our friends, in those who listen, in
those who care. Your active presence in our lives makes our
way bearable and even joyful knowing that you love us deeply.
It is in that joy that we find the strength to make a difference
in this world. Please fill us with your Holy Spirit today and in
the days to come. In Jesus' holy name we pray. AMEN.

Psalm 37:11 (see also Matthew 5:5)

All-powerful God, when we hear the word meek in our society we think of weakness and being easily exploited or bullied. This is because we are taught that only those who dominate will have success. But you who have all the power in the universe, chose to reveal yourself in the weakest of all, a tiny baby born in a manger into a family at the bottom of society. With the guiding of your Holy Spirit, help us to realize that meekness in the sense of the psalm is not lack of strength but rather recognizing that our strength lies in union with you. Our power comes not from reliance on our own thinking but from trust in you. We are our best selves when we seek and follow the direction of your Holy Spirit. In Jesus' name we pray, AMEN.

Psalm 39:1-3

O great Comforter my heart aches. It has taken me a long time to be able to write something on Ahmaud Aubery, another unarmed Black man gunned down, his precious life snuffed out. The Psalm moved my spirit to reflect on how Black people are always called on to suffer in silence. But anger is a flame and it burns. You know my heart and how painful each unnecessary violent death is to me. I can only imagine how much more pain you feel when your people harbor such hatred. I want to scream but it will do no good. I speak out to those who hate people of color, but they don't care. I seek your Holy Spirit to keep me from falling to pieces. I can sit with this a while and grieve, for Ahmaud Aubery, for his family, for the country where this is allowed and even encouraged to continue. But you can lift this from me, so I can return to life, hoping that things will change, praying that those who hate will somehow learn to love. Cover us all with your wings of hope and comfort, for your grace heals. AMEN.

Psalm 42:1-2

Great Provider, we know that water is vital for life. You are the fount of living water and yet we thirst. Why is this? Why do we thirst when you give us everything we need in abundance? Could it be that we don't know you? We search for you but do not see. We seek you but do not notice you. We ask when will we see the face of God and fail to see you in our neighbor, in the beauty of the forest, in the food you supply, in the voice of a child, in the kindness of a stranger. Please break us out of our self-serving bubbles and instill in us your Holy Spirit.
Free us to be with you, and quench our thirst through our living, faithful to the Way of Jesus our Lord and Savior. AMEN.

Psalm 46: 10-11

O God, we have been forced to be still and we have found you in so many ways.
Please continue to send forth your Holy Spirit and encircle us with your love.
We thank you for showing up in the strangest places.
In the bubbles that form when we wash our hands,
In distant waves from neighbors we haven't seen in ages,
In the earthworms making rich soil where we plant,
In a stunning clear blue sky,
In laughter from a game night shared on Zoom,
In the smell of cooking bacon or fresh strawberries,
And so much more...
We are truly grateful for your constant presence and this blessing within the need to shelter in
place - an opportunity to notice! AMEN.

Psalm 47

You are indeed ruler over all nations. Our earthly kings and leaders would do well to turn to you. We pray today for those leaders. Bless them and send your Holy Spirit to release them from the bondage of greed, systemic racism, and pursuit of power. Give them wisdom and compassion to rule for the good of all. Open their hearts and minds to the plight of your people. Let them truly see and empathize and sympathize with those who are at the margins, those who suffer, those who have no voice, those who struggle to live. We will do what we can to lift up our brothers and sisters, to try to break down systems that oppress, and to be your presence to everyone we encounter. It is your Holy Spirit that sustains and guides us. We pray in the name of Jesus, the Christ, AMEN.

Psalm 66: 16-20

Awesome God, we are truly grateful for your steadfast love and generosity toward us. You have sent us your Holy Spirit to dwell within us and surround us with grace. We know you do not reject our prayers because you do not reject us. Our prayers are our connection with you, our relationship with you. You are faithful. It is we who stray from time to time, yet you always welcome us home. You have provided all we need. We praise you with every fiber of our being. Let us feel empowered by your Spirit to love you back by sharing your love with all we encounter, with all of your creation. AMEN.

Psalm 73:16-17

God of understanding, how foolish we are to think that we are capable of anything without you! We seek your Holy Spirit in our lives to guide and teach us. As we try to make sense of this pandemic and the challenges we are facing because of it, we turn to you. Help us to see our way more clearly, help us to recognize how we are to be a positive influence, help us to see where our care is needed, and help us to see the movement of your Holy Spirit in the midst of it all. Thank you for your active presence in our lives and for the good we have in this time of turbulence. In Jesus' name we pray, AMEN.

Psalm 86:11-13

God of Truth, we acknowledge your saving grace and constant love. We want to be true to you, but we struggle to know the way. Even though Jesus has shown us, we fumble along. Living in such a rich and free country has made us slip. We forget who created it all. We forget whose we are. We take things for granted. We pretend everything is all right in the world because it is all right for us. We pause today and remember. We ask you to fill us with your Holy Spirit, as we turn to you. Let us see ourselves in your image. Help us this day to seek your way again, to live each and every moment to honor you, to seek you in everyone, to let your compassion be ours. We ask in the name of Jesus, the one we claim to follow. May it be so! AMEN.

Psalm 90:1-2

God, beyond space and time, you are indeed God, the
One who is, who was and always will be. Your Holy Spirit
permeates all that is created. We cannot escape your goodness
and generosity. We are humbled by the vastness of your love.
Your children, latecomers in the scheme of creation, bow
before you in gratitude for your constant help and grace. You
have never failed us and you are here for us now.
We can endure, we can prevail, we shall overcome. AMEN

Psalm 95:1-7

God of Justice, we sing your praise. We acknowledge your
goodness. We know you are creator and provider. We claim
you as our shepherd. But like the psalmist writes, if only
we would listen to your voice. Today your voice cries out as
always for justice for the poor, the marginalized, the weak and
voiceless. We must listen, we must hear. We invite your Holy
Spirit into our being so that we might be the bearers of your
truth to the world. Our goal will be to help bring justice into
a world that sees injustice as the way of life. We will care for
your people especially those who are invisible in this broken
world. AMEN.

Psalm 100

O Most Holy God, we are weary. This time of sheltering in place has worn us down. We long to be free. We want our lives to go back to normal. Yet, in this time we have learned that slowing down is good, that reconnecting with our families, friends, and neighbors is a blessing, and that when we remove the polluters, the earth cleans itself. Because the most severe disease disproportionately affects communities of color we have had greater awareness of how systemic racism is at work in our country and people were able to respond in protest. We also acknowledge that we have a lot of work to do to make this world safe for everyone. So maybe our eyes have been opened. Thank you for your presence. Please let your Holy Spirit live in us and move us to a better normal. Let us find the absolute joy of living as your people. We belong to you and you know what is best for us. Help us all to realize that your way, the way of justice, the way of kindness and caring, the way of true community is the way of peace and well-being. AMEN.

Psalm 107: 4-9 (see also Matthew 5:6)

O God, our Mother-Father we hear the words 'hunger and thirst for righteousness' and are tempted to soften them by making it solely about personal striving. But in desiring righteousness we must be attentive to the real presence of hunger and thirst affecting humankind. Your Holy Spirit, so alive in us, fills us with such great love that feeding and giving drink to those in need is natural. Seeing pain and suffering becomes part of who we are and doing what we can to alleviate those hardships is second nature to a people who love God. We hunger and thirst for you, O God of love, and righteousness is what follows. AMEN.

Psalm 118:1-4

O God we are not alone. Your steadfast love is forever and constant. We can't escape the reach of your love. As this pandemic lingers and we are trying to regain our footing we give ourselves into your care. We look to the holy scriptures to see your constant sustenance and faithfulness to your people. Throughout the ages you have been our guide and nurturer. We trust in you now. We see your Holy Spirit in action in the world. May it move us and strengthen us as we go forth transformed into this unknown future. Help us to do our part to make a difference for others as well as ourselves, to the betterment of our society and our world. AMEN.

Psalm 126:4-6

God of the suffering, you know our troubles. The pandemic
has brought struggles we never thought would happen to
us. Besides the obvious sickness and death, we are suffering
emotionally, physically, and mentally beyond the viral infection
itself. We experience stress, insomnia, worry, and uncertainty.
All of these things are compounded by the inability to be with
loved ones. We are grateful for your constant presence and
steadfast love even as we fail to turn to you. Please fill us with
your Holy Spirit and illuminate us. Remind us that in our
suffering you are right beside us. Help us to lean on you for
support and comfort. Replenish and restore us. Heal us. Give
us renewed and strengthened faith. These are the fortunes that
last and make the rest of our lives whole. AMEN.

Psalm 126 (see also Psalm 80)

Eternal God, today we lift up all those who have lost their jobs
and insurance. We are experiencing damage to our economy
that is hurting countless people. Many small businesses are
closing their doors, people are running out of resources. People
can't pay their rent and are facing eviction. Food insecurity is
on the rise. We ask, like the psalmist, for you to restore what
we have lost. God please restore our fortunes by opening the
hearts of all who can make a difference and let us all support
each other through these hard times even if it means sacrifice.
Let the pandemic open our eyes to the insanity of our runaway
capitalism and give us a sense of community that will show a
world that reflects your kin-dom. AMEN.

Psalm 128

Awesome God, we honor you. We offer ourselves to you
with reverence and respect. Our current understanding of
fear doesn't work for us. We don't want to be afraid of you,
but we do stand in awe of you. It is amazing that you love us,
sinners that we are. But you do! Your love is extraordinary and
complete. You have given us commandments to guide us on
our path. You ask us to walk with you, to obey for our own
good. The psalm addresses a cis male but we all receive your
promise of happiness, well-being, and prosperity in whatever
form it takes. You love and care for us all. No one is left out.
Bless us with your Holy Spirit as we live and work and relax
in a very different world, in the midst of a pandemic. Open us
to your spirit of grace and pure love that you offer abundantly
and without reservation. We pray in Jesus' holy name, AMEN.

Psalm 136:1

Holy God, you are our source of certainty in a time of confusion and doubt. Here we are, after months of sheltering in place, just now gingerly stepping out. We are weary and anxious about our future. We are afraid to go out, afraid to stay put, unsure about our safety if we venture out, terrified that we could lose our ability to care for ourselves. Mostly we are afraid for those who are more vulnerable. We pray for those who have had or currently have Covid-19. Will they have immunity? Will they have a mild or full-blown case? Will they survive? Is the virus going to be coming around again? Or never leave? There are so many reasons to be scared. But your Holy Spirit is our source of life. We look to you for solid ground when everything seems to be unstable. We look to you to be our foundation. You keep us steady, you center us, so we can see more clearly. You offer grace in a shared cup of coffee online, in a call or card from a relative, in the sweet face of children, in getting through a day of Zoom meetings, in the chirping of birds, in the greening of the earth, in decreased greenhouse gases, in vibrant community worship in the virtual space, and so much more. Open us to your Spirit, to notice, find joy, be surprised and receive your grace even through the chaos and uncertainty. With gratitude for your steadfast love we pray, AMEN.

Psalm 139: 1-4

All-knowing God, everything that has been known, is known, or is yet to be known has its origin in you. You are the beginning and the end. What is astonishing is that you know me, little ol' insignificant me. The vastness of your love allows you to know and love me and care about me always, even in mundane things like when I sit or stand, think or speak. You truly know me and that makes me important, significant, beloved. It overwhelms and brings great joy to my heart. It also gives me reason to trust and rely on you. You have chosen to have relationship with humanity. Let us with gratitude receive your Holy Spirit. May we respond with love and service. AMEN.

Psalm 139: 5-6

Loving Protector, you are all around me. I can feel your presence. It is as a light touch, the sensation one gets from intimate contact with a person who genuinely cares for you. I feel safe, protected, loved, not alone. Your Holy Spirit is a down comforter, soft and gentle on my skin, keeping me warm and secure against the cold things of the world. The chilling emotions of fear, anxiety, and worry accompany the coronavirus. They are very real in my life now, but you calm and soothe me allowing me to face the challenges with confidence. Your love is beyond my capacity to know yet you offer it so tenderly and I find solace and strength in it. AMEN.

Psalm 139: 7-10

Ever-present God, your Holy Spirit accompanies me always.
I may not pay much attention, but she is there. I may be
unfaithful and seduced by the sinful things of the world, yet
you are there to recover me. I cannot hide from you. You will
remain close until I decide to turn to you. If I deny you or
betray you, you forgive me. I cannot run from you for you are
anywhere and everywhere I can go, a constant companion
ready to take my hand and lead me. Your willingness to let
me figure out my own path is a sign of your total love for
me. When I fall you are there to pick me up. When I fail
you are there to teach me and give me wisdom, When I am
lost you are there to give me hope. Thank you, God for your
faithfulness and steadfast love. AMEN.

Psalm 139:11-12

Light Divine, you illuminate everything. Darkness flees when
you are there. When I find myself in darkness, having turned
from the path you set for me, your light returns me to the
way. When I am dragged into dark places by the powers of
the world that would kill and destroy, you rescue me. I cannot
remain in the dark if you are with me. One thought of you
utterly destroys the darkness. With you even the seeming
endless pit becomes escapable. For you are love and your love
heals. Send the light that is your Holy Spirit into us all. God,
please be with anyone who is in darkness and help them to
find that light that lies within them. Heal them, save them.
AMEN.

Psalm 139 :13-18

Great Creator God, you are an artist of the highest degree, one that cares deeply for all that is created. I imagine you sculpting and designing my body in intimate detail, getting everything just so. You made me, just as you wanted me to be. Each creation is special and unique. When we consider the variation and diversity of your created humanity we can see your careful loving hand. Please arouse in us the wonder of your creative hand as we look at each other. With the power of your Holy Spirit give us deeper understanding of who you are by the ability to see you in each person, the mark of the creator who designed each with hope and purpose. Let us feel and know your holy presence in ourselves as well. From our beginning, through our lives and at our end you are with us, all of us. Yes, fearfully and wonderfully made and beloved are we. AMEN.

Psalm 139:19-24

Just and Merciful God, it is hard to look at some people who openly hate and diminish others. It is tempting to wish them gone to keep them from continually harming others. It would be better if they were just not in the world. We know that to hate and hurt is not what you desire, dear God, you who are love. Jesus, whose passion for justice underlies his whole ministry, calls us to love our enemies. That is a tall order. And so we ask you to replace the hateful feelings we might have with thoughts of mercy and concern. We ask for your Holy Spirit to reorder our thoughts with a focus on you. As the Spirit moves us toward union with you, we will find it easier to love even our enemies and pray for them in earnest so that they too will be released from the hatred in their hearts.

My heart feels lighter already. In Jesus' name we pray, AMEN.

Psalm 150

O God our constant companion in life, during the time of trial we often forget that you are with us always. When we find ourselves in times of difficulty – like living in a pandemic – where we see a constantly increasing number of ill and dying, we become enmeshed in sorrow, anxiety, worry, and fear. But even in the midst of all this, you are sending your Holy Spirit over us and surrounding us with your holy grace. The blessings are still coming, though ofttimes overshadowed by pain and suffering. So we stop to tell you we love you and sing praise to the One who never leaves us, who offers steadfast love and a place to rest from exhausting work, emotional strain, and psychological drain.

We praise you with masks and handwashing,
We praise you with social distancing,
We praise you with Zoom and livestreaming
We praise you with creative recordings of music
We praise you with letters and calls.
Let everyone and everything praise you, O God! AMEN.

Psalm 150

Amazing and wonderful God, we praise you indeed; yes all that breathes. It seems relevant especially today when breathing is a challenge. We praise you though it is hard to breathe through a mask. We praise you because you care for those who have shortness of breathe due to Covid-19. We praise you even as a ventilator breathes for some of us. We praise as we find it hard to breathe through smoke of devastating fires consuming so much. We praise you as we find stress and anxiety compromises our breath. Because you breathe into us your Holy Spirit, you add life to our being. We will praise you with every breath and with every fiber of our being. We praise you, O Marvelous God!

The New Testament

The texts from Acts, the Epistles (or Letters), and Revelation offer us insight into the communities that accepted Jesus as the Christ and followed in his way. Acts gives us a look at what happened to the Apostles after the Ascension. In the epistles we find communities just decades after Jesus lived, died, and was resurrected, communities which are as different from one another as the congregations we have today. Those communities faced internal and external troubles. The letters are encouragements, reprimands with corrections, and teaching to the various groups that decided to follow Jesus.

There are beautiful gems in these letters that speak to us today about how we, as followers of Jesus Christ, are identified, how we should live, and what we should know to be good disciples. The Revelation attributed to John was a vision about the world as it should be. It offered great hope to a persecuted church and to us today.

Acts 2:1-4

God beyond all time and space, we yearn for your Holy Spirit
in these trying times. We are tired, anxious, and frightened.
Let your Spirit lift us. Blow on us like wind to stir and animate
your people. Let your love be a growing flame in us. Speak
with us in the universal language of compassion and mercy.
Then, remain with us so that all we do and say will reflect your
grace and love alive in us. In Jesus' name we pray, AMEN.

Acts 10:1 – 11:18

All Powerful God, you pour out your Holy Spirit on the world.
The might of your love overcomes all hatred, all division, all
self-doubt or shame, anything and anyone that would seek
to separate us from you. Your Spirit frees our souls from all
forms of evil, liberates us from bondage and brings us into the
protection and comfort of your holy presence. The immensity
of this inclusive love is beyond our capacity to measure, yet in
your Holy Spirit all can experience the wonder and awe that
comes with being your child. It is with humility and gratitude
that we, as your beloved community, worship, pray, sing, dance,
protest, stand up to bullies, speak truth to power, care for the
stranger, all to praise you and live the life of a follower of your
son our lord, Jesus Christ in whose name we pray. AMEN.

Acts 19:1-22

Great Creator, you are God of all humanity. Your apostle Paul took that to heart by proclaiming your word to his own people and to everyone else who would listen. We live in gratitude that we have known you and have been given the gift of the Holy Spirit. Kindle in us the determination along with the confidence and ability to share your word with others. We may not all be great wordsmiths, but we have experienced your deep and inexhaustible love. Help us to find our own way to let others know the love we have felt from you. Is it in service? Is it in kindness.? Is it in recognizing the humanity of another? Is it a shared note of encouragement? Is it in sharing our testimony with others? Whatever it is, dearest God, help us to be living expressions of your love in the world. We are disciples of Jesus Christ, followers of the Way. We pray in his name. AMEN.

Romans 5:1-8

O God, Wellspring of Life, your people have endured. Despite oppression, war, poverty, dangerous regimes, and natural disasters, your constant and loving presence has always been with us, calming, comforting, and supporting your people. We are facing a new adversary in the form of pandemic caused by a coronavirus which has been difficult to understand and contain. The selfish counterproductive behavior of many with regard to precaution is also very hard to understand. Please let your Holy Spirit fill your imperfect people so we might wear the mask of true compassion. You never withhold your love from us. You even sent your son, Jesus the Christ as our redeemer. O God help us in this scary time. Help us to live Christ-filled lives of caring and sharing. AMEN.

Romans 5:3-5

O God, Our Hope, we, your people have endured centuries of trouble. You have been with us every step of the way. Now that injustices are being acknowledged by more and more people, we ask you to keep your grace flowing into each heart so that we can all understand that when some of us experience pain, suffering, or oppression, it affects all of us. God thank you for the movement of your Holy Spirit in our time and space! You, too, have shown endurance with this country built on racism. It is hard to let go but we can do it! The character of our society may well be shifting. Our young people are speaking to us; they want a country where systems of oppression are identified and destroyed. They want a world where justice rules, your justice in the form of love. O God, though you have poured out your spirit continuously on us, we may now be ready to be moved. In Jesus name we pray, AMEN.

Romans 5: 6-8

God, who persists even when we turn away, we are grateful for your love and grace. We feel that love so deeply when we gather at the Lord's table in communion. It is in those moments that we truly toss out all the egotism, racism, sexism, ageism, prejudice against any based on ability, ethnicity, identity or orientation and just find unity in you. Please let your Holy Spirit fill your imperfect people so we might realize what Christ did for us. Your love gave us the way and in Jesus we have been given a new life. Let us live our lives at the communion table, in unity, in love, with you, seeing all people as your beloved children. Help us to find in ourselves compassion, mercy and love for all creation. AMEN.

Romans 6:1-11

Beloved God, as your children we ask you to send your Holy Spirit into us and open us to your word. Because we are committed to Christ, we have the means to choose life over sin. We are struggling as a nation with the sin of racism. We can choose to embrace it, ignore it as if it will go away, or we can join Jesus and oppose all that would be contrary to your vision of shalom. Jesus knew poverty. He was, and he always will be in solidarity with the oppressed, the unloved, and the voiceless. So how can we who have died to sin go on living in it? Loving God, we need you to break our hearts open, so we can love as you love, see all people as your children, and build each other up rather than tear each other down. In this way we choose life over death, love over hatred, and praise you, honor you, and show our love for you. In Jesus' name we pray. AMEN.

Romans 8:14-17

God of love, God of life, we open ourselves to your Holy Spirit as family, related to each other and you. What an amazing thing that through Jesus we are gifted with your Holy Spirit and we belong to you! Let us be your legacy. Through us let us show the world how wonderful and giving you are. Through us let the world know your compassion and mercy. Through us let the world know you are God and a very present help, showing up in all situations. With the help of your Holy Spirit and the guidance of our lord Jesus Christ, may we show the world what it means to be yours. AMEN.

Romans 8:37-39

O ever-present God your constancy and faithfulness fill my soul with such joy that I am overwhelmed. Your Holy Spirit dwells within me and when I pay attention I find a clarity of purpose and a calm that allows me to focus my energy on the task at hand. Your love is vast and all-encompassing and when I yield to it I find I am more myself than I could ever be on my own. I also am very aware of those around me, connected to me in your love through Jesus. Your grace so abundant reminds me that I am part of your whole creation. My desire is to be open to your Holy Spirit and live my life aware that we cannot be separated. To be one with you is to be one with the creation, connected, caring, complete. AMEN.

Romans 12:4-5

Holy One, a difficult lesson we are learning from this time of pandemic is the inequity in our world. It has been there all along but this infectious agent, so tiny, has destroyed many lives, not because it is a vicious killer but because we as a world have allowed many to be vulnerable. We have left so many without means to stay safe. We who are privileged to have homes, plenty of food, clean water, and health care have forgotten that there are so many who do not, or we simply ignore that fact. We have turned a blind eye toward them or actively stood in the way of their progress. We can help, we can make a difference, but we don't. In fact, we have laws and systems that cause and then exacerbate the situation.

We confess our complicity in this and ask for your forgiveness. Please stir us up with your Holy Spirit so that we no longer behave or think in this way. Let us be the church, the ones who are the Body of Christ in the world, the ones who take to heart Jesus' message of justice, the ones who follow his clear instructions on how to live as members one of the other. It is in Jesus' name that we pray. AMEN.

1 Corinthians 11:23-26

God of Grace, we hear the words of institution each time we share Communion but today the words strike powerfully. Jesus gave himself fully, body and blood, even after being betrayed and denied and he called it a new covenant. We are in this together, we are bound to you through our Lord, Jesus Christ. We never walk alone, we never struggle alone, we are never abandoned. This is the hope you give even when all seems lost or broken beyond repair. In this time of uncertainty and fear we are grateful for your constancy and your deep abiding love. We pray in the name of Jesus, the Christ, AMEN.

2 Corinthians 4:7-12

God of life, we hear that clay jars, something useful but easily broken, can hold a valuable treasure. In this time of pandemic this message is most pertinent. Our bodies are under assault by a highly contagious virus and many are infected. It reminds us how fragile we can be. But the treasure within, your Holy Spirit, is alive and well. It is you, not us, who have power. The beauty of this passage for today is that we have this power within us to be steady and strong in the face of the assault. While some of us will succumb to the disease, you provide the courage to face it. You give us hope and encouragement as we do what needs to be done in order to fight. It is a powerful witness that even in death your presence, this blessed treasure within us, is life! O God help us to rejoice in your Holy Spirit dwelling within us, a gift that helps us to be alive in Christ, even in the face of affliction or possible death. To you be all power and glory forever! AMEN.

Ephesians 4:4-7

God, Parent of us all, we acknowledge your greatness, your majesty, your presence encompassing all there is. It brings awe but also comfort when we consider that you are above all, in all, and through all. We are the body of Christ called into being by the love you shared in Jesus. In this time of upheaval, we ask you to fire us up with the power of your Holy Spirit to be all we can be, using the gifts you have given to each of us. We are all affected by the pandemic in one way or another. Please reveal to us ways in which we may serve you and our neighbors with love and kindness. In faith we will persevere, together as one. In Jesus name we pray, AMEN.

1 Thessalonians 1: 1-10

God of Grace and Peace, there are many around us who have heard the message of your gospel and are moved to live guided by the teachings of Jesus. Filled with your Holy Spirit may we, too, find a sense of conviction in our faith, so that your message of love and inclusion and compassion is lived out in our daily actions and words. We are being tested during this time of pandemic and social unrest. We have a choice to serve others or to be selfish. Our faith reminds us that we can trust you to be with us through the trials. Our job is to remember we are yours and that your way of compassion and love is the way we choose as we follow Jesus. Being like Jesus and his followers may be challenging but it is the right way to live. AMEN.

1 Timothy 6:17-19

Generous Provider, we should be doing good always but in this time of great need it seems that your message to care for others strikes at the core of who we are. We are grateful for the many things you provide that help us through this time of shutdown in the face of the spread of the coronavirus. Please empower us with your Holy Spirit to see the needs around us and to use our wealth to relieve the pain or struggle. Ease our fears so that we can give sacrificially and in love. We put our trust in you. In Jesus name we pray, AMEN.

Hebrews 6:19-20

O God our Hope receive our gratitude for Jesus. He revealed you to us. He opened our eyes to truth. He brought the good news – that you are our God who loves and cares for all. He taught us that we belong to one another. He taught us that we must care for one another. As we move from day to day, help us to recognize our common humanity and understand the profound meaning of being your children, beloved and capable of loving. As we find our way through this time of dramatic change in our world, we ask that you embrace us with your Holy Spirit and move us to be bringers of hope. Hope lies in our receiving and sharing your love. AMEN.

1 Peter 1:3-9

Creator God, a new birth into a living hope is just what we
need. We are so very grateful for this spectacular selfless gift.
Jesus, through his total obedience and love for you ushered in
a new way of living, where justice is foundational, and hope
is eternal. Loving Creator, in our gratitude we open ourselves
to your Holy Spirit. Fill us with hope so that we may be
instruments of hope in this broken world. Free us from the old
ways of living and guide us to your way. In Jesus' name we pray.
AMEN.

1Peter 5:6-11

Force of Life in the Universe, we are so grateful for your
presence! It is calming, encouraging and supportive in this
time of uncertainty and shifting reality. Our nicely formed
world views are being tested, reshaped, and at times shattered
by this experience. And so we come to you, in gratitude and
love because you put the pieces back together, though perhaps
in a different way. You remind us who we are, and you care for
us with a love surpassing all we can even imagine. You remind
us that we are all connected, to you, to each other, to the earth,
and yes, to all creation.
It is with this understanding and inspired by your Holy Spirit
that we pray deeply for all those who are impacted by the
pandemic, which is all of us. We pray especially

• For the sick and their families, those who are caring for
them.

- For those who are in vulnerable situations.

- For everyone going to work or school in-person and not knowing if they will be safe.

- For those who are unwilling to sacrifice even a little for the whole.

- For those who are going through this and feeling alone in their home space.

- For all those essential workers who have kept everything going like they always do.

- For the those who don't have the safety net of savings.

- For those who have mental illnesses, and for all those who are finding it extremely difficult to cope.

God, we know we will struggle with this for a long time but we also know you are suffering with us because of your deep and abiding love. It is a fact that we can rely on you. We put our trust in you. In Jesus' name we pray, AMEN.

1Peter 5:8-10

God our Rescuer and Preserver, these times are so confusing, and quite frightening. We are in unchartered waters, with conflicting leadership and no clear path forward. In times like this we are wise to admit that we cannot go it alone. It is when we are most vulnerable that the evil in the world becomes a threat. In our weakness we can be lead astray. We seek the guidance and support of your Holy Spirit. Let the movement of your Spirit in us give us comfort and calm, wisdom and understanding, and fortitude and perseverance for the days ahead. We know that you will not abandon or desert us in our need. Strengthen our faith as we face great difficulties in our lives. We trust in you to deliver us. Give us the courage to help others, to be your hands and feet in a time of suffering. We pray in the name of Jesus who suffered but endured, AMEN.

Revelation 1:8

O God our Source, we come from you and we return to you. The amazing thing is that you are with us throughout the journey. We need only turn to you and you are there. You are at our beginning, through our growth and development, through every trial, through every joy, through our doubt and in our surrender. It is our deepest desire to experience your Holy Spirit intimately and fully. When times are difficult, like now, we need you more than we admit or realize due to worry, anxiety and uncertainty. We ask that you open our eyes and ears and hearts and minds to your Spirit. Move us to let go, to feel the natural pull toward you and rejoice in your willingness to love us as we are and as we may become. AMEN.

Revelation 21:1-4

O God who abides with us, you are our God and we are your people. Surround and permeate our lives with your Holy Spirit. Be with us in this time of trial, in our communities, in our work, in our daily walk. Change is upon us. It seems the old is passing away. Help us to make the most of what we are learning through this difficult time. Open our hearts and let us be contributors to a new earth. Let your vision of the world move us to be a more just society, one that values all its citizens. Give us grace to make your vision our vision for the whole world seen through the lens of Jesus Christ in whose name we now pray, AMEN.

Other Sources for Reflection

During this time of the pandemic, I have found myself drawn again to some helpful quotes from people whose writings or speeches I have come across during my time in seminary or in personal study. I have included verses from the **Gospel of Thomas** which is a gospel referenced by the church fathers in the 3rd century and rediscovered in 1945 in Nag Hamadi. It is dated to around 60-100 CE. This gospel is a collection of sayings attributed to Jesus and carries on the tradition of Jewish wisdom sayings. It is Jesus' vision for what humanity can attain, what we are to be. The sayings predate the synoptic gospels and parallel them. These particular sayings have resonated with me in this time.

*I have often been moved by **Saint Teresa of Calcutta**. Mother Teresa's ministry to the poor is an outstanding example of obedience and caring. The inspirational quotations I have included here have often guided me in my own life and I use them in my work.*

*__Martin Luther King Jr__ and his mentor **Howard Thurman** are important sources of reflection for me.*
Their understanding of the worth of people being God-given has guided me and helped me through many a trial. Naturally their words would come to me again as I fight fear and anxiety in this scary time that has once again revealed the unequal status of marginalized communities due to systemic racism in this country. This has been highlighted by the disproportionately higher levels of severe Covid-19 illness in people of color, the poor, and those with limited health care resources. Dr. King's beloved Community is the same marginalized community Jesus lifted up.

*__C.S. Lewis, Harold Kushner__ and **Dietrich Bonhoeffer** have contributed poignant theological reflections on many topics, including suffering and pain as part of the human condition and our misplaced values. Such writings are particularly germane to pandemic times. There are many writers who give testimony to God in their lives. Ruminating on the words of those whose faith brought them to share with others is another way to connect with the God we love. God touches us in so many ways. God is good.*

Thomas 25

Jesus said; Love your brother as your own soul.
Protect him as you protect the pupil of your eye.

God, you who love us dearly, we hear Jesus' words to love one
another and to protect our neighbors with the voracity that we
would protect our own eyes. This is so important today as we
shelter at home to protect those who must be out, and those
who cannot survive this disease. To imagine that we can see
all our siblings in Christ as we see ourselves is so radical in a
society of 'me first' individuals. But that is what Jesus says. This
is teaching from the Hebrew Scriptures, love your neighbor as
yourself. We have heard this from Jesus before. Here we find
him likening it to the automatic and instinctive protection of
our eyes. O God, please help us with the power of your Holy
Spirit, to protect each other instinctively out of love as Jesus
taught. AMEN.

Thomas 27a

If you do not fast from the world, you will not find the kingdom.

Holy Presence, here we are in a season of uncertainty and our circumstances with the coronavirus have forced us into a fast from the world as we knew it. We ask you to shower us with Your Holy Spirit and bless us in this time of retreat from the world as we knew it. In giving up our control, let us put our trust in you. In giving up our freedom to come and go as we please, let us find you where we are. In giving up our routines, let us not be anxious but rather creative. In giving up the way we do things, let us find joy even in the process of finding new ways. In giving up a privileged sense of safety, let us do what we can to make ourselves and others safe. We are grateful for your presence in the world and this opportunity to notice. AMEN.

Mother Teresa of Calcutta :

"If we have no peace, it is because we have forgotten that we belong to each other."

Holy One, Source of peace, we turn to you once again to bathe in the comfort of your presence. When you offer shalom, your peace that passes understanding, you offer wholeness and wellbeing. As we care for ourselves and those in our communities in physical isolation, let us not forget about those beyond these boundaries. We belong to each other and we recognize that all of humanity's brokenness, suffering, and pain is our own, shared by you. We know that through your Holy Spirit you heal. So, we ask that you pour out your enormous healing power over the world. Heal us, O God, make us whole, give us courage to do what we can and give us strength to give over to you what we cannot. AMEN.

Mother Teresa of Calcutta: another prayer inspired by –

"If we have no peace, it is because we have forgotten that we belong to each other."

God of All, this quote resonated in me when I heard and spoke the chant "No Justice, No Peace" at the peaceful protests across the country. For it is the truth that in you we belong to one another. It is the basis of our living in you. You are in relationship with us all and that makes us related through you. You are our loving Creator who cherishes the creation. We are family; you are the father/mother/parent and that makes us brothers and sisters. Justice is required because when some are oppressed, we are all affected negatively by that oppression. It is our calling to build up rather than tear down, love rather than hate, protect rather than ignore. We fervently ask you to bring your Holy Spirit into your family, the body of Christ, and move freely and with immediacy to make us the united loving family you want us to be. Peace is possible with your love guiding us to equal justice for all. AMEN.

Mother Teresa of Calcutta :

*"We think sometimes that poverty is only being hungry,
naked and homeless. The poverty of being unwanted,
unloved and uncared for is the greatest poverty.
We must start in our own homes to remedy this kind of
poverty."*

God of the poor, you are with us in the wilderness during
this time of pandemic, thrust into a time of unknowing and
uncertainty. It is here where we find ourselves face to face with
you, asking us to be faithful. Caring for the poor, those on the
margins of society, is the mark of being your people. In this
pandemic it feels even more important to follow that way of
being, beginning with those who are alone or cut off from their
family and friends because of the safety measures put in place.
Ever-present God, please move your Holy Spirit in all of us to
think of those who are alone, who might be feeling unwanted,
uncared for or unloved. We ask you to bless each of them
through us. Hold them in your care. Your love is everything.
We gratefully receive it and we will share it. AMEN.

Martin Luther King, Jr.:

"We must accept finite disappointment but never lose infinite hope."

O God hear us! We hang our heads in shame that our nation has oppressed so many for so long. This is the richest nation in the world, but we treat our poor abominably. The pandemic has only served to highlight the injustices we ignore because we benefit from them. This virus does not choose one victim over another, but it is clear that those who live on the margins, who have been deprived of position in this country by racism or poverty have little means to secure themselves. The rest of us depend on them to put themselves at risk to keep us safe. With little healthcare insurance they will suffer disproportionately, more likely to have underlying illness, poorer nutrition, and less time for self-care. Those who don't put themselves at risk on the job are at risk because they don't have the luxury to be off work for 2 months. They live paycheck to paycheck and their safety nets are at risk by our leaders who take what little they have to give to the already rich. We recognize this, and we know, dear God, that the answer is there before us. Those who have must help those who do not. This is your vision and desire for the world. So, we ask to you to start with us and give us the fullness of your Holy Spirit to destroy our old world view and replace it with your world view. Let us see each and every person on the earth as a sibling and friend. Give us the courage to be willing to stand with the poor and oppressed among us. Give us the determination to help others thrive. Then move the world to do the same by the healing power of your love. O God hear our prayer. AMEN.

Martin Luther King, Jr. from
Letter from Birmingham Jail:

"Injustice anywhere is a threat to justice everywhere. We are caught in an inescapable network of mutuality, tied in a single garment of destiny. Whatever affects one directly affects all indirectly."

God of justice, during the pandemic systemic racism is on display in the unequal severity of disease in the marginalized, in the unequal treatment of persons of color and in the fact that many of those called on to put their lives at risk are those same persons who are experiencing injustice already. It is out there evident for everyone to see. The injustices that serve to prop up the dominant culture and oppress the rest are manifest in this heavier burden upon those persons. As followers of Christ we have learned that it is justice that defines us as your people. We ask you immerse us in Your Holy Spirit to increase our awareness of the connectedness we have with you and with one another. We must fight for justice every day of our lives. When one of us suffers we all suffer. When one of us is oppressed we are all oppressed. Freedom requires justice. Peace requires justice. AMEN.

Howard Thurman:

"In whatever sense this year is a new year for you, may the moment find you eager and unafraid, ready to take it by the hand with joy and gratitude."

"There must be always remaining in every life, some place for the singing of angels, some place for that which in itself is breathless and beautiful."

God, most beautiful and gracious, we are awestruck by the magnitude of the abundant and overflowing grace poured out on us each and every moment. This is cause for chest-bursting joy, a feeling of overwhelming gratitude for your presence in our lives. These words of Howard Thurman often find their way to my consciousness when I am feeling burdened, shaken, lost, or scared. I can connect with you in one breath, the joy of your being there is enough to gird me. I can hear you in music or find you in the vast number of shades of green I see in the trees and shrubs. We all have those special God-moments we cherish. If we pay attention, we can hear that still small voice (or perhaps it is a booming voice!) that is in our deepest being telling us we are your beloved children. Awareness of these things turn the impossible into your possible. Please, open the hearts of all your beloved and give us that joy that will not be shaken by anything. Let us drink from the well of joy that is your Holy Spirit, to be steadied, held, or fortified. We pray in Jesus' holy name AMEN.

Howard Thurman:

"Don't ask what the world needs. Ask what makes you come alive and go do it. Because what the world needs is more people who have come alive."

God of the Universe, it is you who makes us come alive because when we each follow your plan for us we become energized and find our true selves. In a time of pandemic, it is easy to fall into worry, to forget the gifts and blessings you have bestowed on us that will help get us through. We struggle because we try to face it alone. But when we turn to you we are reminded of our strength in you. We ask that you saturate our souls with the steadiness and wisdom of your Holy Spirit. Help us to see the way even in these confusing and chaotic times. Help us to come alive in you! AMEN.

Howard Thurman:

"Listen to the long stillness: New life is stirring. New dreams are on the wind. New hopes are being readied: Humankind is fashioning a new heart. Humankind is forging a new mind. God is at work. This is the season of Promise."

Faithful and Constant Holy One, you are indeed at work, you always are. Howard Thurman's words are a powerful statement to our present situation in this time of pandemic, in this time of enlightenment. The time of sheltering offered us a stillness, and out of that we have found a new life in the hope for justice and equality. We are able to dream again, and it seems that more are along for the ride. God, we thank you for your Holy Spirit in these times, the movement of your spirit certainly has stirred something in the hearts of thousands who have taken to the street and many more who have joined the cause in other ways. How astonishing that even in the midst of a pandemic your love can shine through! Justice is a sign of your active presence. Thanks be to you, great God of love. AMEN.

Howard Thurman in Jesus and the Disinherited:

"Wherever his [Jesus'] spirit appears, the oppressed gather fresh courage; for he announced the good news that fear, hypocrisy, and hatred, the three hounds of hell that track the trail of the disinherited, need have no dominion over them."

God of all, God of the oppressed, we know that in Jesus there is hope and that we can gather courage in him. We see in the sin of racism the hatred brewed over the past 400 years that will not die even as we work tirelessly to change that situation in our country. Today we are afraid of the unknown with this virus and the way it continues to spread, especially among those harmed also by racism. We are shaken by the hypocrisy we see in those leaders at whose mercy we find ourselves. As your Holy Spirit flows in flames of love over and around us, let the spark within us burst into a fire that gives us strength and courage to continue the work in the face of these great challenges. We who are bound to Jesus pray in his holy name. AMEN.

Howard Thurman in Meditations of the Heart
(his prayer in italics)

Open unto me — light for my darkness.
Open unto me — courage for my fear.
Open unto me — hope for my despair.
Open unto me — peace for my turmoil.
Open unto me — joy for my sorrow.
Open unto me — strength for my weakness.
Open unto me — wisdom for my confusion.
Open unto me — forgiveness for my sins.
Open unto me — tenderness for my toughness.
Open unto me — love for my hates.
Open unto me — Thy Self for my self.
Lord, Lord, open unto me!

God of blessing, in your mercy send your Holy Spirit to open our hearts and minds to your great gifts. As we pray this beautiful prayer from Howard Thurman we breathe in your Holy Spirit and accept your gift, breathing out the thing it replaces. Your generous and steadfast lovingkindness makes us whole. In Jesus' blessed name we pray, AMEN.

C.S. Lewis in The Problem Of Pain:

"God whispers to us in our pleasure, speaks to us in our conscience, but shouts in our pains: it is His megaphone to rouse a deaf world."

God, conversation partner, this quote made me ponder how, when we experience pain or suffering due to illness, other problematic aspects of our world may become uncovered. We are in a pandemic and it has affected all of us. While it is true that some of us were prepared to weather the storm, others have been thrown into a state of poverty. Some of us have great insurances should we become ill, while others are unable to seek care and will probably wait longer than they should to be seen. This disparity is laid right out for view. This may be the megaphone Lewis talks about. Are you speaking to us in our communal pain? Why are we able to hear you when we suffer and ignore you when things are good for us even as others are suffering? Loving God energize us with your Holy Spirit to be attentive to your whispers and thank you for shouting through pain especially the pain of others crying out for help. Rouse us to the suffering in the world and stir us to action. AMEN.

Harold Kushner, When Bad Things Happen to Good People:

"God does not cause our misfortunes. Some are caused by bad luck, some are caused by bad people, and some are simply an inevitable consequence of our being human and being mortal, living in a world of inflexible natural laws. The painful things that happen to us are not punishments for our misbehavior, nor are they in any way part of some grand design on God's part. Because the tragedy is not God's will, we need not feel hurt or betrayed by God when tragedy strikes. We can turn to Him for help in overcoming it, precisely because we can tell ourselves that God is as outraged by it as we are."

Compassionate and merciful God, we, like Rabbi Kushner, know that you don't cause these things but rather share our experiences of pain, sorrow, and anguish, all because of your amazing love. You hold us when we are afraid and assure us that you are very much present. We thank and praise you for the gift of your Holy Spirit who pours out your love and grace on us every day. You must be very disappointed with us, since we have been complicit in the unjust systems that caused the vulnerabilities of so many of our brothers and sisters in this pandemic. Thank you for opening the eyes of so many in these months. There is a movement toward justice that could only happen because you are in the world. Move us all to be compassionate and caring. Give us the fortitude and perseverance to continue this work toward a just world. In Jesus' name we pray, AMEN.

Dietrich Bonhoeffer:

"Christianity preaches the infinite worth of that which is seemingly worthless and the infinite worthlessness of that which is seemingly so valued."

Creator God, we find ourselves in the middle of a pandemic, one for which we were not prepared. As we try to contain and end it we are staying home from work and activities outside the home and trying to figure out a new way of living our lives until this threat is ended. This quote from Bonhoeffer reminds us that we should value life and our connectedness with you and each other over material possessions and money. Our claim to Christianity has become an individual acceptance of salvation without the life of service Christ preached. In this time with the virus raging we are forced to look at what we truly value. Some cry "my rights!" saying that they have the right to gather for worship and refuse to help the common good by wearing masks or keeping distance. It seems disingenuous to claim Jesus and not care about the people around you. O God, it is hard not to judge these people. I ask you to fire us up with your Holy Spirit so that we value the lives of all and safety for all and that we be willing to sacrifice to make it so. Open the hearts of all your people. AMEN.

Scripture Index

USING THE REVISED COMMON LECTIONARY, LETTERS A, B, AND C INDICATE THE CYCLE YEAR IN WHICH THE TEXT APPEARS.

Key Words

Anxiety:
> 2, 13, 18, 20, 46, 47, 51, 52, 66 ,70 ,71 ,85 ,88

Black Lives Matter:
> 45

Black, Black and Brown, People of Color:
> 3, 8 ,56, 61, 88, 95

Covid-19:
> 1, 21, 65, 71, 88

Fear:
> 2, 13, 14, 18, 20, 22, 31, 41, 47, 50, 51, 52, 55, 64, 66, 68, 70, 80, 82, 88, 99, 100

Hope:
> 7, 8, 12, 13, 18, 19, 24, 29, 33, 34, 39, 40, 49, 51, 54, 56, 67, 68, 73, 76, 80, 82, 83, 94, 98, 99, 100

Injustice:
> 3, 11, 18, 23, 42, 44, 45, 60, 76, 94, 95

Justice:
> 6, 12, 17, 19, 23, 30, 32, 42, 44, 45, 60, 61, 69, 76, 79, 83, 92, 95, 98, 102

Pandemic:
> 7, 8, 12, 14-17, 19-21, 28, 29, 32, 33, 35, 37, 38, 42, 46, 51, 52, 54, , 59, 62-64, 70, 76, 79-81, 83, 87, 88, 93-95, 97, 98, 101-103

Peace:
> 3,4, 11, 33, 42, 45, 61, 81, 91, 92, 95, 100

Praise:
> 21, 24, 35, 37, 44, 46, 55, 58, 60, 70, 71, 74, 77, 102

Protest:
> 11, 12, 27, 45, 61, 74, 92

Racism:

> 3, 12, 14, 17, 19, 22, 32, 45, 54, 58, 61, 76, 77, 88, 94, 95, 99

Safe:

> 8, 10, 27, 38, 42, 45, 49, 54, 61, 65, 66, 79, 84, 90, 93, 94, 103

Suffer/Suffering:

> 6, 8, 15, 16, 18, 19, 21, 28, 42, 50, 54, 56, 58, 62, 63, 70, 76, 84, 85, 88, 91, 94, 95, 101

Trust in God:

> 8, 20, 21, 25, 27, 29, 30, 32, 33, 39, 44, 46, 51, 52, 56, 62, 66, 81, 82, 84, 85, 90

Uncertainty:

> 2, 18, 31, 34, 41, 63, 65, 80, 83, 85, 90, 93

Virus/Coronovirus:

> 1-3, 8, 12, 13, 22, 32, 39, 48, 54, 65, 66, 76, 80, 82, 90, 94, 99, 103

Worry:

> 20, 46, 47, 63, 66, 70, 85, 97

Extrabiblical Sources

RESPONSES TO SPIRIT PRAYERS:
PRAYING THROUGH THE PANDEMIC AND SOCIAL UNREST

Devoree Crist's Spirit prayers make a stairway for the heart to climb up from this time of pandemic fear and need for justice. They will continue to be a source of strength and grace for individuals and groups in the days to come.

– Rev. Maren Tirabassi, Author and Pastor.

In Spirit Prayers 2, Devoree Crist offers more well-crafted prayers that are in careful conversation with biblical material and keenly sensitive to the current painful realities of the pandemic and the pervasive racism of our society. These prayers will both instruct and inspire.

– J Clinton McCann, Professor

Excellent work. Well done. Great thoughtfulness and reflection on scripture. A good follow up to Book 1.

– Rev. Clyde R. Crumpton, Pastor

Dr. Devoree Clifton Crist is a spiritual director,
retired physician, wife and mother living in St. Louis, Missouri
She holds a Master in Theological Studies from Eden
Theological Seminary and a Graduate Certificate in
Spiritual Direction from Aquinas Institute of Theology.
She received her doctorate degree from Washington University
School of Medicine in St Louis.
During Covid season her retreat ministry has halted,
but, in its place, a very rich and fruitful
group spiritual direction ministry has emerged.
The pandemic has allowed for creativity in and enjoyment
of virtual worship liturgy and music,
painting and, of course, writing.